ARGENT SOFTWARE SIMPLY SAFE SERIES

SECURITY SOLUTIONS FOR AWS

Understanding Network Security
and Performance Monitoring
for Amazon Web Services

Published by Argent University

For more information, please contact:
www.Argent.com

ABOUT THE ENGINE ON THE COVER: The iconic 500cc BSA Gold Star engine was manufactured by BSA from 1938 to 1963. Four stroke, air cooled, and alloy construction, it was one of the fastest production motorcycles of the 1950s.

TABLE OF CONTENTS

INTRODUCTION

One of the 20th century's leading economists provided what has turned out to be the most durable definition of capitalism; according to Schumpeter, capitalism is Creative Destruction.

And Amazon Web Services is a perfect example of this creative destruction.

AWS has radically changed IT and the changes are mostly beneficial. There are some hidden areas that do require special care. And some of these critical hidden areas are described in this book.

☁ ☁ ☁

What makes AWS so much better than its competitors is simple—dog food.

The common IT expression of "eating your own dog food," or using the tools you created, is never more apt than with AWS.

AWS started as an internal solution at Amazon as a reaction to Amazon being unable to find a decent cloud solution. Yes, it is true that many software vendors had created a range of mediocre and tawdry cloud products. But these products were typical of so many products from so many software vendors: unstable, inflexible, unable to scale, and—most important of all—pompous.

Of all human activities, few can match the pomposity of software vendors, staffed as they are by introverts who often speak—but rarely listen to—customers. And their cloud products are perfect examples—products that so-called designers have promulgated from on high for the laboring masses.

In direct contrast, AWS was created by the people truly at the front line, not nattering nabobs cloistered from the real world.

This is what makes AWS so effective—it is used every day by people in the real world who want to sell books online. And this real-world capability makes AWS stand head-and-shoulders above its competitors.

This small book may help you in understanding and implementing and expanding your use of AWS.

If you would like to speak to an Argent AWS expert, please access **www.Argent.com**

Sincerely,

Andrew Blencowe
President and CEO, Argent Software

FIVE PITFALLS OF AWS

EXECUTIVE SUMMARY

"The earlier you see and deal with a problem, the smaller it is. The later you see and fix a problem, the bigger it is."

This fundamental precept applies to everything you do. With respect to cloud computing, you can use this precept to save time, save money and achieve greater uptime and availability. Managing your company's IT resources to ensure both the lowest possible expense and the best possible customer experience is often a difficult balancing act. Renting IT services from a cloud vendor (such as Amazon) can be helpful, but you have to constantly monitor cloud services for unexpected outages, software errors, and performance issues.

Your disaster recovery plan—which you should always have at hand, ready to use—also needs to have a Plan B, an alternative that you can turn to when Amazon Web Services stop, slow down or misbehave.

Quickly finding out that you have a problem with your cloud data storage, cloud Web hosting or cloud remote computing is the first step toward solving that problem.

Amazon cloud-based facilities are, unfortunately, out-of-sight and out-of-reach. However, you can easily run monitoring software that closely watches your cloud services for problems. The monitoring software gives you early notification of errors, difficulties, slowdowns and imminent failures.

PITFALL 1: AWS OUTAGES

AWS has suffered many outages over the past few years.

A cloud is just someone else's data center that you rent time and space from. It's not magic, and it certainly isn't perfect. Amazon Web Services (AWS), like all other clouds (and all other data centers, for that matter), is subject to a wide range of problems—connectivity failures, software errors, and hardware malfunctions. AWS experiences all of these from time to time.

On June 5, 2016, a storm-related outage denied network access and computing services to Australian AWS customers for more than six hours. The unavailable AWS services included Elastic Compute Cloud (EC2), Relational Database Service (RDS), Database Migration Service, Elastic Beanstalk, and several others.

On September 20, 2015, a five-hour outage disrupted access to several popular online sites, such as Netflix, Tinder, Airbnb, Reddit and IMDb. The outage also halted a number of Amazon's own services, including Prime Instant Video. Amazon later admitted that a software error at its US-EAST-1 data center in northern Virginia had caused the outage. The software error triggered faults in 24 AWS services, ten of which crashed and died.

Note that Netflix was able to rapidly thwart the effects of the five-hour September 20, 2015 outage. Netflix used a monitoring tool to quickly detect the problem, and it implemented a disaster recovery plan that switched its customers to other data centers. Netflix had replicated itself across multiple data centers in anticipation of just such an outage.

A hardware malfunction on April 20, 2011 brought several AWS services to a standstill. A disk array controlled by Elastic Block Store (EBS) stopped responding to read/write commands. The outage lasted more than two days.

A storm of epic proportions (which local people would later refer to as "the inland hurricane") disrupted access for many hours to the northern Virginia AWS data center on June 29, 2012.

Software issues caused major AWS outages on October 22, 2012 and on December 24, 2012. The October 22 outage, which affected sites such as Reddit, Foursquare, Pinterest, and others, was the result of a memory leak programming error. A different programming error, in the Elastic Load Balancing service, caused the December 24 outage.

Another long-duration northern Virginia AWS data center outage, on August 10, 2015, interrupted access to many popular Web sites. The affected AWS services included Elastic Compute Cloud (EC2), Elastic Beanstalk and Simple Storage Service (S3). Amazon reported that "a configuration error in one of the systems that Amazon S3 uses to manage request traffic" caused the outage.

Other recent AWS outages of varying durations occurred on the following dates:

30 August 2016	22 August 2016	16 August 2016
29 July 2016	19 July 2016	20 June 2016
9 June 2016	2 June 2016	21 April 2016
30 March 2016	10 March 2016	2 February 2016
25 November 2015	19 November 2015	18 November 2015
15 October 2015	14 October 2015	

Does AWS host your company's Web site(s)? Store your company's data? Run software to update or analyze your company's information? Your disaster recovery plan needs to explain, in detail, the steps you take to switch temporarily to an alternative. The alternative might be slower than you'd like, or it might be function-limited, but having that alternative can save your company a great deal of money and loss of goodwill.

First and foremost, however, you must run a monitoring tool to get early detection of AWS outages.

PITFALL 2: AWS PERFORMANCE PROBLEMS

A good monitoring tool identifies bottlenecks, measures resource utilization and reveals what's happening inside the otherwise opaque AWS cloud.

Performance issues in the cloud are notoriously difficult to troubleshoot and solve. The fault might be related to a hardware malfunction, a programming error, a network change, a system configuration error, a lack of resources or, sometimes, just high traffic levels.

You may suspect that AWS itself has slowed down when in fact the problem is in the tangled web of network connections between your site and the AWS site. For example, a Tier 1 Internet backbone pro-vider (such as AT&T, CenturyLink, Cogent Communications, Level 3 Communications or NTT Communications) might re-route traffic around a broken cable (backhoe equipment operators sometimes dig holes in the wrong places). A misconfigured router in any tier of the Internet can cause slowdowns. And a hacker can launch Distributed Denial of Service (DDoS) attacks that flood parts of the Internet with traffic or that specifically target Internet resources essential to your cloud connection (such as a DNS server).

Amazon rents a variety of computing resources to its AWS custom-ers. Prices naturally increase as you choose faster CPUs, more mem-ory, faster disk access and greater bandwidth. But you always have to keep in mind that you're sharing the cloud computer(s) with other Amazon customers—the responsiveness you might see early Sunday morning, when the computers are not very busy, will be distinctly different from the sluggishness you might experience in the middle of the afternoon on a Thursday.

Specifically, Amazon uses hypervisors to create virtual machine (VM) instances in which your software runs. You rent one or more VM instances from Amazon. Note that hypervisors themselves can become quite busy creating, managing and destroying VM instances. On a physical machine running many VMs, hypervisor overhead can sometimes impede VM instances from using the CPU or from access-ing necessary resources.

Software running inside AWS can suffer unforeseen slowdowns if CPU utilization, disk I/O, memory usage or network traffic/latency exceeds what you've allocated. All too often, you're faced with a combination of these situations.

CPU utilization problems can sometimes be solved by reprogram-ming (optimizing the code), by splitting up the workload and running multiple instances of the software (perhaps with the help of AWS' load balancing service) or by allocating more AWS "Elastic Compute Units" (ECUs). In simplest terms, Amazon says one ECU is equal to the computing speed of a 1.0 GHz to 1.2 GHz Intel CPU. Use your monitoring tool to alert you when CPU utilization is high.

AWS Elastic Block Store (EBS) is a popular service for storing files on disk. EBS gives you large capacity disks on network-connected block storage devices. Be aware that, from a performance viewpoint, EBS slowdowns occur when the rate of I/O requests is greater than the storage devices can accommodate, when network traffic between the computers and the storage devices is high (other AWS customers may be competing with you for disk I/O on the same devices) or when the "chunks" of data to be stored or retrieved are greater than 16 kb in size. EBS is optimized to handle 16 kb data blocks.

An application crashes and dies when it completely exhausts its AWS-allocated memory. You can add swap volumes to your AWS instance to sometimes cure an out-of-memory condition. However, because the operating system uses the swap volumes to page memory blocks to and from disk, performance suffers. Disk I/O is orders-of-magnitude slower than memory access.

If you have a transaction-oriented application that runs out of memory in high-traffic situations, you might consider having AWS run additional instances of the application, via Elastic Load Balancing (ELB), to handle the occasional high workload. Such scaling is quite common on AWS.

Use your monitoring tool to track memory usage and take steps to avoid application memory exhaustion. Note that if ELB scales your application based on traffic levels, you should also track latency for ELB instances. Load balancing operations can cause considerable network activity (and thus latency), sometimes in a cascading fashion.

You can also track such statistics as:

- The number of requests that could not be properly load-balanced (caused sometimes by a lack of healthy servers to which ELB can route extra traffic)
- Web requests per minute
- The number of healthy Web servers in the load balancer pool

PITFALL 3: AWS DATABASE ISSUES AND DISPARITIES

AWS RDS database services (such as DynamoDB, ElastiCache, Elastic MapReduce, Redshift and the cloud versions of the relational databases MySQL, Oracle, SQL Server, and PostgreSQL) are subject to issues and troubles beyond the typical ones that you see when you install and use one of these database products in your own data center.

Each RDS instance is a version of the database product running as an AWS EC2 virtual machine instance on an EC2 platform. It uses AWS EBS volumes for data storage. You have no access to the underlying EC2 instance, and you do not get access to S3 in order to "see" or otherwise process your stored database snapshots. On the other hand, AWS creates on-demand database snapshots for you (extra storage charges apply), and AWS Automatic Backup promises point-in-time data recovery that's no more than five minutes old.

You also cannot install software running alongside the database product. This restriction precludes you from using an agent-based monitoring tool to keep watch over your database operations. Make sure the monitoring tool you buy doesn't need to install an agent on the database server.

AWS does not allow you direct access to database configuration files, but rather exposes an API that you can use to configure the database.

Some of the facilities of the database product, such as replication, are not available in the AWS cloud. Furthermore, you have no access to transaction logs or the MySQL binary log.

AWS does not allow you to act as Supervisor or Administrator of your database. This means, for example, that you cannot manually shutdown the database (as you would be able to if the database server were located in your own data center).

Network latency can dramatically affect your database updates, retrievals, and queries. For any database operations you perform over the Internet from your site, the cloud-based AWS database is by definition going to be less responsive than a database server that sits in your own data center.

PITFALL 4: AWS FAULT LINES

AWS has a number of other idiosyncrasies and deficiencies you'll want to be aware of.

DNS Security—A Domain Name Service (DNS) cyber-attack can replace the correct IP address for a URL with a substitute IP address that redirects people to a fake server. The spoofed Internet address is often a Web server whose Web pages look like those of a legitimate bank or a popular online merchant. The IETF's Domain Name System Security Extensions (DNSSEC) protocol thwarts such attacks by using digital certificates and private keys to establish DNS name server trusted sources. Note that AWS supports DNSSEC for domain registration but not for regular, ongoing DNS name resolution. If you want to use DNSSEC for a domain registered with AWS Route 53, you must use a different DNS service provider.

Latency-based Routing—AWS Route 53 doesn't support ecdn-client-subnet DNS extensions, a protocol that's especially useful for geographically-dispersed content delivery. These extensions forward the higher part of the client IP address to the authoritative DNS server for the specific purpose of latency-based routing.

IP Address Assignment—Avoid assigning (or even needing to know) IP addresses. You can then use AWS load balancing to automatically scale up (or down) as appropriate, and you can disperse your application across multiple AWS availability zones.

AWS Service Limits—Amazon enforces a variety of limits on customer activities. Be aware of these by reviewing AWS service limits before you begin using AWS. If AWS notifies you that you've exceeded one of these limits, you can email a request to AWS technical support asking that the limit be increased, but you don't want your AWS processes to sit in an idle state while you wait for AWS support to act. Monitor your AWS usage and make your service limit increase requests before you reach a limit. Note that some of the limits are AWS-global, while others are region-specific.

PITFALL 5: "AMAZON WILL DO IT ALL"

Like all new technologies, AWS is seen as a panacea, as a cure all. While AWS does provide many benefits and introduces useful new features and facilities, it is still just technology, with all the limitations that implies.

Chief among these limitations is the wishful thinking that Amazon addresses all the AWS issues. While it is true that Amazon has done a superb job with AWS, in the final analysis, it is the customer who must implement a complete and comprehensive monitoring and automation facility that is completely independent of AWS itself.

Argent for AWS is a uniquely powerful solution, engineered as a completely new product, from the ground up, not simply a tarted-up lash up.

Argent for AWS has a number of unique features, including:

- Complete support of AWS Console and AWS SDK
- Comprehensive alerting via Argent Console
- Long-term trend analysis (not just AWS's 14 days)
- Native OS monitoring of Windows and Linux
- Native monitoring of applications on Window and Linux
- Complete S3 monitoring
- Integrated log monitoring of S3, EBS, and EC2

For a free 30-day evaluation of Argent for AWS, please send an email to Sales@Argent.com

2

SEVEN SECRETS OF AWS SECURITY

EXECUTIVE SUMMARY

Security is a pain in the ass.

It is that simple, and this is why so many computing systems are so vulnerable: people are lazy. There is a clear, inverse correlation between security and convenience—good security is truly a pain in the ass, and—moreover—extremely expensive. Good security is expensive because people have to jump through so many additional hoops.

And good security needs excellent IT management, which is generally lacking. Far too often IT "management" seems to consist almost entirely of attending the latest Gartner seminar to be willingly indoctrinated in the latest fad; "bi-modal" is the current fad-of-the-week.

A practical example from the real world: a few years ago when the Web was the Bright New Thing, lazy programming managers (who would never dream of reading their programmers' code), allowed even more lazy programmers to scrap the screen for a password and to plop it directly into a SQL query, allowing even the dullest hacker to simply add a second query to the string. Sad.

Like on-premises virtual machines before it, AWS is very much a two-edged sword. When adding a new server consisted of trucking in a 25-ton behemoth to a specially prepared computer room, planning was exhaustive and exhausting. Today, it is three minutes work from a mobile phone, and today's server is a 100-fold more powerful than the ancient behemoth.

With this dangerous informality, all too often little or no thought is given to security—"Amazon will do it." Wrong. Dangerously, catastrophically wrong.

It is highly likely that most AWS EC2 implementations are far less secure than the on-premise ones they replace.

Want proof? A recent study found over 1,000 misconfigurations in EC2 instances per AWS account.

This chapter provides a simple check list for AWS security. Like everything in life, nothing is free. It is the main responsibility of competent IT management to strike the appropriate balance with respect to convenience versus security.

SECRET 1: WHO'S ON FIRST; NO, WHO'S ON SECOND

Geeks—and all-too-often, their managers—love new toys.

As AWS is the newest and brightest new toy, everyone wants a piece of the action. And now! In this haste, no proper management structure is created for the mushrooming AWS implementations, and *this is especially true of the only really critical management role—AWS Security Czar.*

The best way of implementing this is to start by creating an AWS Security Department. Yes, a department through which all AWS implementations and security changes must pass. This team of security specialists has two goals: to vet ongoing changes and to constantly preach to all AWS admins the **dangers** of AWS.

Admins, like programmers, will cut corners when they know they can get away with it. The specialist AWS Security Department must be the stern mother, not the always-indulgent father. As AWS has an ever growing list of features, so security training must never end.

SECRET 2: LOGS

Far too many admins create EC2 Instances and fail to turn on all the logging. Sometimes this is sloth, but more often it is simple ignorance. This is especially true for neophyte AWSers who mistakenly believe just creating the EC2 Instance is sufficient.

But AWS CloudTrail is essential (and it's often useful for debugging as well). CloudTrail provides a chronological log of all AWS API calls, and records the identity of the caller, the caller's IP address, parameters and the values returned by the AWS service.

In a word, CloudTrail is gold-dust.

And the CloudTrail logs can be readily and automatically checked by a number of third-party products, such as Argent for Compliance.

In addition, CloudTrail logs can be boiled down to provide extremely effective trend analysis and capacity planning.

One of the odd quirks of CloudTrail is that it cannot be turned on retroactively—this is yet another reason for the creation of the

AWS Security Department: to prevent these dangerous creation oversights.

SECRET 3: TOO MANY WITH UNNECESSARY PRIVILEGES

Without a formal plan and catalog of who has what privileges and why, security rapidly collapses, and needlessly allocated elevated privileges are granted to far too many people.

Worse, there is never any review of why an admin has so many elevated privileges.

Worse still, there is often no automated daily report of newly departed employees that maps to their AWS rights and privileges. Countless studies have shown long-departed former employees still holding all the keys to the castle.

This is where the AWS Security Department described in Secret 1 is a lifesaver.

"External auditor" is often defined as "those obnoxious know-it-all outside accountants who come in and tell us everything we are doing is wrong." Good. In some cases the traditional outside auditors do find genuine errors; in all cases, the threat of periodic visits by the persnickety auditors keeps the in-house accounting staff on their toes.

The same goes for admins—the AWS Security Department needs to conduct quarterly security reviews of every admin with any access to AWS. Very effective and very much a pain in the ass—good security is not cheap.

And all security requests need to be vetted by the AWS Security Department; this is how the chronic problem of IT's laziness can be corrected once and for all.

SECRET 4: SILOS OR DEATH

Good security requires planning and *following the rules*. In the Battle of Jutland, the British lost *Queen Mary* and *Indefatigable*, both disintegrated after being hit by German shells because the most basic rule of Action Stations—all water-tight doors being dogged—was ignored. When the more-accurate German shells rained down on both ships, the resultant flashes ignited the cordite in the magazines. Rules are there for a purpose.

The "water-tight doors" of AWS is silos.

Design multiple accounts and multiple Virtual Private Cloud (VPC) definitions—isolate workloads and independent teams.

Of course, testing, development, and production must be in separate, hermetically-sealed silos.

SECRET 5: NO ENCRYPTION

This is a no-brainer.

All RDS (Relational Database Service) and EBS (Elastic Block Storage) must be encrypted.

There can be no debate; "it is part of our AWS standards" is the refrain that every admin must know by heart.

SECRET 6: PASSWORDS ARE TOO CONVENIENT

A very good rule in all security designs is: Easy = Bad.

This is actually a corollary of the first line of this chapter.

Many large companies—prestigious companies—companies that should (and probably do) know better, rely solely on passwords.

AWS has a rich array of optional facilities, such as two-phase authentication and physical cards. Sadly, these are optional and the lazy approach is the good old password.

In five or ten years, just using passwords will be illegal; the EU has been moving in that direction since August 2015.

Two-phase authentication must be the standard; passwords alone will not suffice.

Of course this also addresses the madness of the "passwords" of '12345', 'secret', 'none', etc.

SECRET 7: INSTANTLY FIRE ANY ADMIN USING 0.0.0.0./0

Napoleon said, "After I execute one of my generals, all the others fight much better."

The same goes for any admin who uses 0.0.0.0/0. Using 0.0.0.0/0 allows any machine anywhere—think Russia or China—the ability to access your AWS resources.

AWS Security Groups can be used as wrappers around and EC2 Instance to police both inbound and outbound traffic; use them. And make them stern and severe—if in doubt, No!

For all remote access, always use a Bastion Host to provide an added layer of security (A Bastion Host is an EC2 Instance that acts as a clearing house; see https://en.wikipedia.org/wiki/Bastion_host for a good introductory description.)

One excuse sometimes heard is the need to patch "on-the-fly." Patching on-the-fly is like repairing a plane's wing while the plan is flying. Don't. Rather create a new image and a new Instance and apply the patch to this new Instance.

WHAT MAKES ARGENT FOR AWS UNIQUE

EXECUTIVE SUMMARY

This chapter provides background information on the AWS Console, details of the new Argent for AWS product, and a brief matrix of the marketplace, as well as explaining what features make Argent for AWS unique.

The Amazon AWS Console already provides some monitoring features through CloudWatch and Service Health Dashboards; this chapter explains what is lacking in the AWS Console.

As far as the marketplace is concerned, it seems most competitors are simply doing a small subset of what AWS Console does, and integrating with their own data-center monitoring suite.

The following table is a summary of the leading products:

	Argent	BMC	ManageEngine	SolarWinds	Nagios
CloudWatch	Yes	Yes	Partially	Partially	Partially
EC2 (AWS)	Yes	No	Yes	No	No
EC2 (OS)	Yes	No	No	No	No
EB App	Yes	No	No	No	No
RDS	Yes	No	Yes	Yes	No
DynamoDB	Yes	No	No	No	No
S3	Yes	No	No	No	Some
SimpleDB	Yes	No	No	No	No
Custom Metrics	Yes	Yes	No	No	No
Zero Footprint	Yes	Yes	Yes	No	No

Most competitors simply monitor EC2 instances and only through CloudWatch.

Though EC2 service is popular, it is only one of 36 CloudWatch namespaces.

For a complete list of all CloudWatch namespaces, see Appendix B.

1: CAPABLE OF MONITORING ALL ASPECTS EXPOSED BY AWS CONSOLE AND AWS SDK

One critical feature is Custom Metrics.

Application developers can use the AWS API to expose any performance data deemed important to CloudWatch. The namespace, metric and dimensions are up to the developer.

Argent for AWS implements the generic CloudWatch Rule, which behaves similarly to Windows Performance Rule—with Argent, users can browse, select and monitor any available CloudWatch metric including Custom Metrics.

2: INTEGRATED WITH ARGENT CONSOLE, THE WORLD'S LEADING ALERTING CONSOLE

The available alerting and escalation mechanisms are years ahead of the modest email and SMS services provided by AWS.

3: INTEGRATED WITH ARGENT PREDICTOR FOR LONG-TERM TREND ANALYSIS

Argent performance data is not subject to a 14-day limit (all AWS data is deleted after 14 days).

4: CAPABLE OF MONITORING OS NATIVELY

Both Windows and Linux are supported.

The performance data gathered directly from OS is typically more trustworthy than external CloudWatch metrics.

CloudWatch on EC2 provides the following metrics:

- CPUCreditUsage
- CPUCreditBalance
- CPUUtilization
- DiskReadOps
- DiskWriteOps
- DiskReadBytes
- DiskWriteBytes
- NetworkIn
- NetworkOut
- NetworkPacketsIn
- NetworkPacketsOut
- StatusCheckFailed
- StatusCheckFailed_Instance
- StatusCheckFailed_System

These metrics cover the basic CPU, Disk I/O and Network Traffic, and a few are AWS-specific.

Compared to the rich array of Windows Performance Counters (often exceeding 5,000 on a large server), the AWS statistics are very much first-generation and bare bones.

5: CAPABLE OF *NATIVE* MONITORING OF WINDOWS AND LINUX *APPLICATIONS*

Typical diagnostic data, such as service/daemon status, CPU utilization, memory usage, handle count, Windows Event Log, file-based application log, etc., are all available for monitoring with Argent for AWS.

Example 1: Monitor a Web Application

Assume a web application is implemented in .NET, that it consists of two web front-end servers, a mid-tier application logic server, and SQL Server, and that there are a total of five EC2 Windows instances.

Using the AWS console, the only metrics that can be seen are that the five EC2 instances are in good health, which means hardware and OS are running properly.

But in this example the web servers are generating hundreds of 500 and 404 errors every minute.

This is unknown to the AWS Console.

Using the AWS console, there is no way to detect any *application-level errors*, such as:

- Is the IIS service down?
- Mid-tier application crashes
- SQL Server database runs out of space, or excessive queue lengths

In direct contrast, *Argent for AWS can determine the root cause* using Windows Service Rule, Windows Performance Rule, Windows Event Log Rule and Windows File Log Rule on SQL error log etc.

Using the AWS Console to monitor applications is like trying to monitor a Windows web server's applications using SNMP.

Yes, very broad brush strokes, such as ping alive and CPU busy, can be tested, but no detailed application-level metrics are available.

Example 2: SQL Server EC2 Instance

The AWS Console can only provide information on whether the Windows EC2 instance is up.

It has no visibility on health of the internals of SQL Server.

On the other hand, Argent for AWS can answer all the following questions:

- Is SQL Server service running?
- Does SQL Server run out of space?
- Did user authentication error happen?
- Are there too many concurrent users?
- Are there excessive disk queue lengths?
- Are hard page faults ballooning?
- Is CPU usage too high?
- SQL Server deadlock issue happens?

6: COMPREHENSIVE S3 MONITORING

Instead of treating S3 as a flat structure of individual buckets, Argent for AWS monitors S3 as a typical file system.

This is a vital technical point. According to Forbes, 97% of users use S3 service. See Appendix A.

AWS Console provides almost zero monitoring capability.

Argent for AWS can monitor S3 in the manner similar to monitoring Windows NTFS. The following are some examples:

- Alert can be fired if an object is modified in the past 5 minutes
- Alert can be fired if a folder contains more than 300 objects
- Alert can be fired if a folder size (sum of all objects in the folder) exceeds 1 GB

7: COMPLETE LOG MONITORING ON S3, EBS VOLUME OR EC2 INSTANCE STORE VOLUME

AWS has CloudWatch Log service doing typical keyword searching or matching.

However, it requires installing a separate agent on every EC2 instance.

The configuration is not user friendly, and requires direct editing of the configuration files.

Argent has decades of experience in handling logs.

Argent for AWS is superior in all aspects for integrated log monitoring.

AWS BASIC CONCEPTS

EXECUTIVE SUMMARY

The cloud services business is massive and is growing like a weed. For customers moving to AWS or Azure, it is simply a matter of how much and when—it is no longer "if".

This chapter is a tour d'horizon of the current state of AWS.

As Heraclitus rightly observed *"Only Change Is Constant,"* so AWS and Azure are both likely to evolve rapidly over the next 10 years.

COMMON AWS ABBREVIATIONS

S3	Simple Storage Service
EC2	Elastic Compute Cloud
EBS	Elastic Block Store

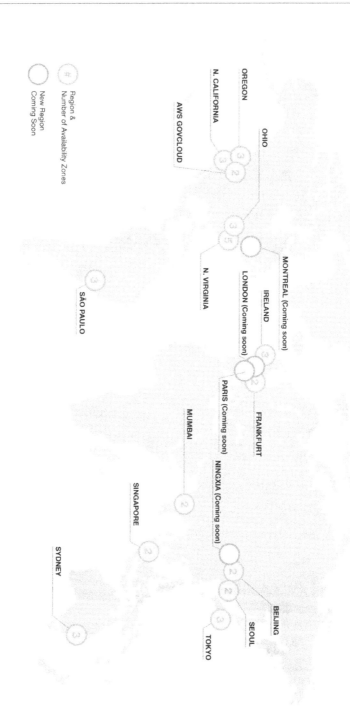

Source: https://aws.amazon.com/about-aws/global-infrastructure/

RDS	Relational Database Service
ELB	Elastic Load Balancer

AVAILABILITY REGIONS

AWS currently operates in 38 "Availability Regions" in 14 different geographic locations, as the map at left shows.

In each Availability Region there are one or more Availability Zones, which is simply a fancy name for an industrial-strength data center—redundant everything. In addition to Availability Regions, AWS also has dozens of Edge Locations. These are specialized, lightweight servers that cache data closer to the end user, decreasing network hops.

AWS CONSOLE

This is the console to *manage* Amazon Web Service (AWS).

It can be compared with VMware vSphere.

See CloudWatch below for *monitoring* AWS.

ELASTIC EC2 INSTANCES

These are Linux or Windows virtual machines running in the cloud.

They are essentially standalone servers in the DMZ.

EC2 Instance = Linux or Windows machine.

Over 65% of EC2 Instances are Windows machines and this percentage over Linux is increasing.

In most respects EC2 can been seen as akin to Rackspace and other service providers.

Studies show that most AWS customers spend at least 70% of their AWS investments in EC2.

EBS—ELASTIC BLOCK STORE

While most EC2 instances come with local disks, these disks only exist for the life of the instance, that is, the existence of the virtual machine.

For permanent storage—for such things as databases—AWS customers use an Elastic Block Store, which is persistent.

SECURITY GROUP

This is similar to a hardware firewall. Security Groups control the allowed in/out traffic to EC2 instances.

CLOUDWATCH

This is the AWS performance metric facility.

It can be compared with Windows Performance Monitor, or more similarly, to Performance tab in VMware vSphere.

A performance metric is defined by:

- Namespace, which can be compared to Windows Performance Objects.
- Metric, which can be compared to Windows Performance Counters.

- Dimension, which can be compared to Instances for Windows Performance Objects.

CloudWatch performance metrics are only kept for 14 days.

ELASTIC BEANSTALK APPLICATION

This is a facility to deploy and monitor web applications.

It can be compared to a typical web farm with load balancers, web servers, and backend servers, but put under a single umbrella.

This is similar to an Argent Enterprise Application Object in Argent AT.

SIMPLE STORAGE SERVICE (S3)

It is the AWS cloud storage solution. It can be thought of as Dropbox, Google Drive, etc.

S3 has only two levels:

- **Bucket**—it can be thought of as a drive in the File System
- **Object**—it can be thought of as an individual file in the File System.

There is no real folder hierarchy like a typical file system. All objects are actually directly under the bucket.

To simulate the folder hierarchy, the *object* can have a name like *folder1/folder2/…/name*. The AWS Console organizes objects in the folder hierarchy. But this is just for presentation.

RELATIONAL DATABASE SERVICE (RDS)

AWS provides traditional Relational Databases, including MySQL, PostgreSQL, Oracle, and SQL Server.

A critical difference between an AWS RDS and an on-premises database is control: like many AWS services, customers lose control to gain ease of use and the ability to scale. Thus, fine-tuning the RDS is not available. It is simply pointing the connection code to the RDS IP address provided by AWS.

Of course, the performance might be slower due to internet connection, and the cost might be daunting because of the traffic.

Most importantly, AWS users do not own their database servers. RDS is available and can be assigned by AWS to any location.

DYNAMODB AND SIMPLEDB

They are No-SQL databases. SimpleDB is a bare bone service with zero management, while DynamoDB can be managed in detail.

APPENDIX A

Much has been written regarding how businesses are rapidly increasing their use of Amazon Web Services, including:

- The increase in the number of EC2 instances.
- The increasing Windows-based instances.
- The increasing need for Cloud-based security products, given the movement of data and applications to AWS.

For example, see:

http://www.forbes.com/sites/benkepes/2015/05/22/
how-are-organizations-using-amazons-cloud/#522be8023bce

APPENDIX B

CloudWatch namespaces are containers for metrics. Metrics in different namespaces are isolated from each other so that metrics from different applications are not mistakenly aggregated into the same statistics.

All AWS services that provide Amazon CloudWatch data use a namespace string, beginning with "AWS/." When you create custom metrics, you must also specify a namespace as a container for custom metrics.

The following services push metric data points to CloudWatch.

AWS Product	Namespace
Amazon API Gateway	AWS/ApiGateway
Auto Scaling	AWS/AutoScaling
AWS Billing	AWS/Billing
Amazon CloudFront	AWS/CloudFront
Amazon CloudSearch	AWS/CloudSearch
Amazon CloudWatch Events	AWS/Events
Amazon CloudWatch Logs	AWS/Logs
Amazon DynamoDB	AWS/DynamoDB
Amazon EC2	AWS/EC2
Amazon EC2	AWS/EC2Spot (Spot Instances)

AWS Product	Namespace
Amazon EC2 Container Service	AWS/ECS
AWS Elastic Beanstalk	AWS/ElasticBeanstalk
Amazon Elastic Block Store	AWS/EBS
Amazon Elastic File System	AWS/EFS
Elastic Load Balancing	AWS/ELB (Classic Load Balancers)
Elastic Load Balancing	AWS/ApplicationELB (Application Load Balancers)
Amazon Elastic Transcoder	AWS/ElasticTranscoder
Amazon ElastiCache	AWS/ElastiCache
Amazon Elasticsearch Service	AWS/ES
Amazon EMR	AWS/ElasticMapReduce
AWS IoT	AWS/IoT
AWS Key Management Service	AWS/KMS
Amazon Kinesis Firehose	AWS/Firehose
Amazon Kinesis Streams	AWS/Kinesis
AWS Lambda	AWS/Lambda
Amazon Machine Learning	AWS/ML
AWS OpsWorks	AWS/OpsWorks
Amazon Redshift	AWS/Redshift
Amazon Relational Database Service	AWS/RDS
Amazon Route 53	AWS/Route53

AWS Product	Namespace
Amazon Simple Notification Service	AWS/SNS
Amazon Simple Queue Service	AWS/SQS
Amazon Simple Storage Service	AWS/S3
Amazon Simple Workflow Service	AWS/SWF
AWS Storage Gateway	AWS/StorageGateway
AWS WAF	AWS/WAF
Amazon WorkSpaces	AWS/WorkSpaces

ALSO FROM THE ARGENT
SOFTWARE SIMPLY SAFE SERIES

ARGENT SOFTWARE SIMPLY SAFE SERIES

INSTANT REPORTING

ARGENT REPORTS

CREATE PROFESSIONAL
REPORTS FROM ARGENT
PRODUCTS OR ANY DATABASE
IN UNDER FIVE MINUTES

ARGENT UNIVERSITY

AVAILABLE FROM THESE AMAZON STORES TODAY:

US: www.amzn.com/0947480749

UK: www.amazon.co.uk/dp/0947480749/

AU: www.amazon.com.au/dp/B075VG1ZCJ/

Argent Reports is a robust, web-based reporting product that allows system administrators to C-level management to construct powerful and stylish reports.

The data can be taken from Argent products, or from external sources—typically SQL databases, making Argent Reports a flexible product with an extremely powerful report scheduler.

Illustrated instructions for 30 reports, including:

- SLA Uptime/Downtime
- Performance
- Compliance Best-Practices
- PowerShell Reports
- SQL Query Reports
- Alerting and Incident Management
- Exchange Mailbox and Traffic

INDEX

ABOUT THE AUTHOR:
FIVE PITFALLS OF AWS

BARRY NANCE is a networking expert, magazine columnist, book author and application architect. He has more than 29 years of experience with IT technologies, methodologies and products.

Over the past dozen years, working on behalf of Network Testing Labs, he has evaluated thousands of hardware and software products for ComputerWorld, BYTE Magazine, Government Computer News, PC Magazine, Network Computing, Network World and many other publications. He's authored thousands of magazine articles as well as popular books such as Introduction to Networking (4th Edition), Network Programming in C and Client/Server LAN Programming.

He's also designed successful e-commerce Web-based applications, created database and network benchmark tools, written a variety of network diagnostic software utilities and developed a number of special-purpose networking protocols.

ABOUT NETWORK TESTING LABS

Network Testing Labs performs independent technology research and product evaluations. Its network laboratory connects myriads of types of computers and virtually every kind of network device in an ever-changing variety of ways. Its authors are networking experts who write clearly and plainly about complex technologies and products.

Network Testing Labs' experts have written hardware and software product reviews, state-of-the-art analyses, feature articles, in-depth technology workshops, cover stories, buyer's guides and in-depth technology outlooks. Its experts have spoken on a number of topics at Comdex, PC Expo, and other venues. In addition, they've created industry-standard network benchmark software, database bench-mark software, and network diagnostic utilities.

ABOUT ARGENT UNIVERSITY

ARGENT UNIVERSITY offers free training and educational summits held around the world to help our customers, and prospective customers, maximize their use of Argent's best-in-class network management tools. The curriculum is typically two days in length and attendees are encouraged to bring their laptops as there are numerous hands-on exercises. Topics include:

1. **THE FOUR BUILDING BLOCKS:**
   a. Creating Rules
   b. Alerts
   c. Monitoring Groups
   d. Relators

2. **ARGENT ARCHITECTURE**

3. **CASE STUDIES**

4. **ARGENT PRODUCT TRAINING:**
   a. Argent Guardian Ultra
   b. Argent for Compliance
   c. Argent for VMware
   d. Argent Defender Ultra
   e. Argent Commander
   f. Argent for SAP
   g. Argent for AWS

5. ARGENT REPORTS AND TOPOLOGY
6. MAINTENANCE SCHEDULES

Attendance to each Argent University is free and includes breakfast, lunch and a cocktail hour at the end of each day. Continuing Education Units available based on host location.

Past Universities have been held in:

- Auckland (NZ)
- Brisbane (AU)
- Florida (US)
- London (GB)
- Los Angeles (US)
- Melbourne (AU)
- New York (US)
- San Diego (US)
- Singapore (SG)
- Sydney (AU)
- Washington DC (US)
- Wellington (NZ)
- Zurich (CH)

For more information, please visit:
www.ArgentUniversity.com

www.ingramcontent.com/pod-product-compliance
Lightning Source LLC
Chambersburg PA
CBHW061044050326

40689CB00012B/2973